THE CHANGING

Blackbird L'eys

Carole Newbigging

**SERIES
NUMBER
48**

Robert Boyd
PUBLICATIONS

Published by
Robert Boyd Publications
260 Colwell Drive
Witney, Oxfordshire OX8 7LW

First published 2000

Copyright © Carole Newbigging and
Robert Boyd Publications

ISBN: 1 899536 57 4

Printed and bound in Great Britain at
The Alden Press, Oxford

TITLES IN THE *CHANGING FACES* SERIES

Do you want to publish a book?

It is not as difficult as you might think. The publisher of this book provides a service to individuals and organisations, large and small.

Advice can be given on all facets of book production.

If you have a project you would like to discuss why not contact:

Robert Boyd
PRINTING & PUBLISHING SERVICES
260 Colwell Drive
Witney
Oxfordshire
OX8 7LW

Contents

Front cover picture

The Dressed Pram parade along Blackbird Leys Road,
at the junction with Moorbank, during the Festival of June 1965.

Back cover pictures

The Staff of J E Pill, butchers on Balfour Road, in 1975.
Left to right: Chris Pill, David Hutchinson, Ivan Woodall,
Ian Godfrey and Bob Pill.

Acknowledgements

Many people have helped in providing both photographs and memories, but I owe particular thanks to Dorothy Fox for allowing free use of her booklet *Blackbird Leys: A Thirty Year History;* also to Ealing Family Housing Association for information based on *The History, Landscape and Buildings of Blackbird Leys Farm*. Photographs have been provided by many individuals and I would like to thank Elaine Arnold, Andy Beale, Eileen Clements, Mr and Mrs Deadman, Martin Gaisford, Les Gaul, Mavis Harris, Jim Hewett, Lorraine Higgs, Margaret Howard, Bill Lee, David McNish, Michael Mazurek, Denis Murray, Gordon and Margaret Peel, Nigel Smith, Michael Sneade, Ann Spokes Symonds and Terry Waite (with apologies to anyone inadvertently omitted). I particularly thank David Munday for allowing me use of his own personal photographs of Blackbird Leys Junior School and for his unfailing enthusiasm.

I am most grateful to Keith Price, Picture Editor at Oxford and County Newspapers for permission to reproduce photographs from that library and to Gillmann & Soame for permission to reproduce the 1965 school photograph. Also the Centre for Oxfordshire Studies, Oxford City Council, the Blackbird Leys Parish Council and Helen Shayler for access to parish minutes and papers, James Ramsay and the Church of the Holy Family, the local shops and youth club, and the headteachers of the local schools.

Exploring and finding material for this book has given me the opportunity of meeting many old friends. I hope that others will gain as much enjoyment from reading this book as I have had in putting it together.

My enjoyment was somewhat curtailed by the task of naming the 580+ pupils and teachers in the 1965 school photograph at the end of the book. This soon turned into a marathon, but all efforts were made to correctly name the majority, but I would apologise to anyone who has not been recognised, or incorrectly named.

Foreword

Blackbird Leys, our community, has a very positive story to tell. Yet the estate is often stereotyped, misunderstood and misrepresented. In a world where bad news is more newsworthy than good news, the drama of the negative too easily drowns out so much that is good.

Blackbird Leys deserves to have its story told straight. How it developed and how the community grew. Recognition is overdue for the work that so many Blackbird Leys residents have put into community groups, the schools, the community centre, the churches, the businesses, the clubs and the pubs.

We must remember the community events over the years — from the Qualidays at the Community Centre, which added a new word to the English language, and evenings of fun to the lives of local pensioners — to the Festival and the street parade on a scale unmatched by any other part of Oxford. We must applaud the energy and dedication so many have put into youth groups, the Oxford Blackbirds Football, and charities. Blackbird Leys is not the richest part of Oxford, but it is one of the most generous.

It is good to record too the changing economic fortunes of Blackbird Leys. Periods when it has been blighted by unemployment contrast with the times when there have been plenty of jobs. The changing fortunes of the car industry have always been entwined with those of the estate, still important even as our dependence on it has diminished.

The community has grown by a third with the new development, bringing new changes and opportunities. Few places have coped so well with such an addition to their number.

Perhaps most importantly — and what outside observers most often overlook — is the good neighbourliness which is a feature of so much, if, sadly, not all, life in Blackbird Leys. There are so many wonderful people here. It makes Blackbird Leys somewhere special. This book gives a rewarding view into its heart and history.

Andrew and Val Smith

Andrew and Val Smith have lived in Blackbird Leys since 1979. Andrew represented Blackbird Leys as a City Councillor from 1979 to 1987, and since then as a Member of Parliament. He was, for many years, a governor of Wesley Green school and Treasurer of the Blackbird Leys Festival. He is President of Oxford Blackbirds youth football club and Patron of the Pathway Workshop charity.

Val has represented Blackbird Leys on the City Council since 1987. She became involved in community activity through the PTA at the then Ivanhoe Middle School and the Adventure Playground. She currently represents the Council on the Ealing Family Housing Area Committee, the Neighbourhood Support Scheme and the Tenants Forum. She chaired, for many years, (whilst it was in existence), the Blackbird Leys Development Committee. Val was Lord Mayor of Oxford 1999/00 and Sheriff the following year.

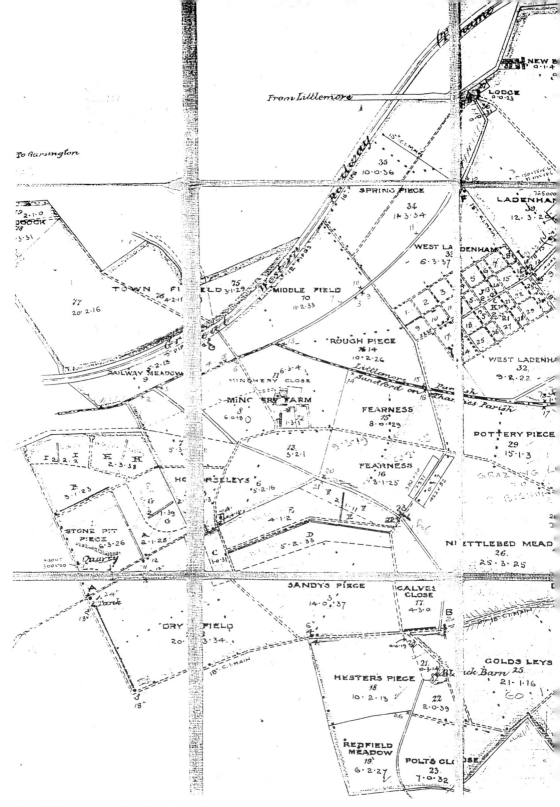

An 1899 map of the Sewage Farm and surrounding fields. Many field names are remembered in present day streets and roads. Ladenham, comprising large fields to the rights, has been retained in Ladenham Road and Sawpit Meadow and Farm in Sawpit Road. Shepherd's Hill and Brake Hill on the right are now parts of the new

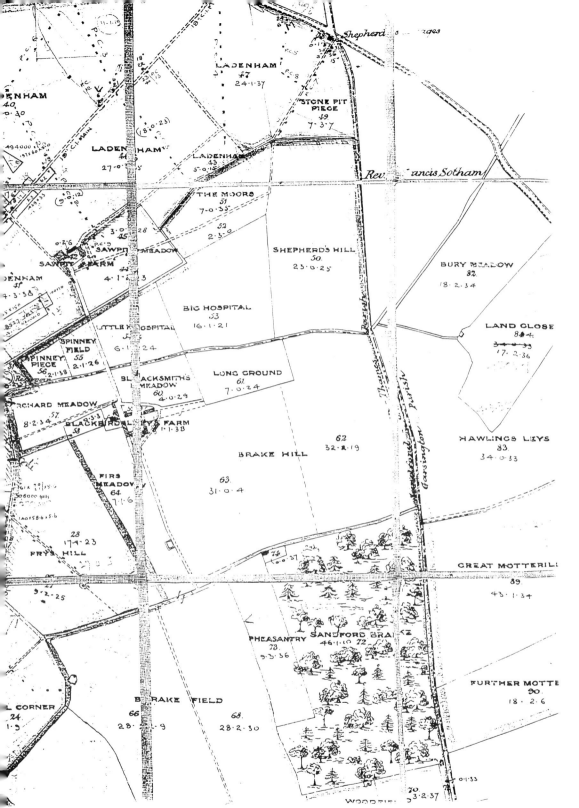

development, as are Long Ground, Frys Hill, Nettlebed Mead and Pottery Piece. In the extreme south is Redfield Meadow, which may have given its name to Redefield School. Orchard Meadow, adjacent to Blackbird Leys Farm, gave its name to the present day First School in Cuddesdon Way.

Oxford City Council draft plan of Blackbird Leys Estate, May 1957.

The first roads were originally numbered one to fourteen, and numbers can still be seen on this plan. Note the proposed site for a public house, on the corner of Tucker Road opposite the stadium. This site was never developed for a public house, but became the site for the Sacred Heart Catholic Church. Note also the second parade of shops on Blackbird Leys Road, now the site of the Community Centre. Further along Cuddesdon Way, on the corner of Sawpit Road, can be seen two Police Houses, now converted into Cuddesdon Corner Family Centre.

Blackbird Leys Farm

Blackbird Leys Farm, as part of Sandford parish, belonged to the Powells. for several generations, a family of staunch catholics. In 1581 Edmund Powell sold off much of the parish, probably including the Farm. The owners of Blackbird Leys Farm, between the 1580s and 1750, are unknown. During this period several families were tenants of the Farm, including the Russell, Woodley, Wood and Powell families. In 1751 Blackbird Leys was described as *'one messuage (house), two gardens, 50 acres of arable land, 20 acres of meadow and 30 acres of pasture.'* At this time it belonged to Edward Sadler, a prosperous farmer, whose family flourished in the adjoining parish of Garsington, from the 1680s to the 1810s. Edward Sadler died in 1787, at which time the tenant at Blackbird Leys Farm was Richard Yeats.

In 1807 Richard Wootten, an Oxford mercer and City Councillor, acquired all the shares in Blackbird Leys, but sold these in 1825 to Richard Costar, coachmaster of Cowley and Oxford. Costar had built a sizeable business and Oxford was a main centre for stage-coaches outside of London. At Blackbird Leys Costar grew oats, beans and hay for his horses, as he did on the nearby Sawpit Farm in Littlemore.

In 1842 his heirs sold the two farms to Christopher Waddell, his junior partner. By the 1850s Waddell was competing with the railways and soon coaching-inns stood deserted and there was no money to be made from stage-coaches. In the census of 1851 the tenant was John Eglestone, farm steward of 413 acres, employing five servants. In 1857 the Waddell family sold the farms to the wealthy James Morrell.

James Morrell's magnificent mansion, Headington Hill Hall, looking down over the City of Oxford, was completed in the year he bought Blackbird Leys. In 1856, the year before the purchase, he had bought five large farms in Culham and had added Sandford Brake Farm of 84 acres to the 326 acres he had inherited at Sandford. A few years later, in 1861, he bought another large farm just across the Garsington boundary to the east. At Blackbird Leys James built new east and north ranges of farm buildings around an enlarged farmyard. He died in 1863, leaving his estates to his daughter, Emily, a minor, in the care of Trustees.

James Morrell's Sandford Estate, including Blackbird Leys, was the home farm for Headington Hill Hall. In 1863 the farm bailiff was William Blackall, the last bailiff being John Gilkes. The Oxford Local Board took over the western part of the Morrell estate in 1877, as a Sewage Farm. In 1895 both Blackbird Leys Farm and Sandford Brake Farm were sold to the City of Oxford. (Based on The History, Landscape and Buildings of Blackbird Leys Farm, Oxford, by David Sturdy, a survey for Ealing Family Housing Association.)

The Farmhouse at Blackbird Leys Farm was built between 1525 and 1580, possibly by Cardinal Wolsey. The house faced south and measured approximately 39 feet by 24 feet, made from thick stone walls, presumably from rubble from the dismantled Nunnery at Minchery Farm. Massive chimney stacks stood at each end, with four main rooms on two floors, with two attics in the roof space. A later wing at the back, of stone and brick, was added about 1750.

The rear of the farmhouse taken in February 1993. The 'lean to', at the rear of the house had been demolished. The last tenant was Mr Harry Dugdale, earlier tenants had included Mr and Mrs Hodnett, whose children attended the newly built Blackbird Leys County Primary School.

The aisled barn in June 1982, which stood at an angle to the south of the farmstead. In July 1982 this building was noted as being an eight-bay aisled barn constructed in elm timber. Although built in the 19th centurey, most probably mid-century, this type of barn was usually found in medieval and early post-medieval building periods. During development of this site the barn was moved to its current position south of Windale Avenue, with a plan to incorporate it into a new City Farm. Sadly this plan did not materialise.

The farmstead in August 1992, during demolition and development. Note the back of houses to the extreme right and the block of flats of Evenlode Tower in the background.

The farmhouse in April 1994. The original intention was to conserve the fabric of the building, and convert or incorporate this old farmhouse into offices for the newly developed Greater Leys. Unfortunately, the building did not survive and was eventually totally demolished. The 'new' Farmhouse on Greater Leys replicates the original as far as possible.

Blackbird Leys Farm viewed from Pegasus Road, 1989. An air balloon had just come down within the farmyard.

A large farmyard, nearly 140 feet long and 70 feet wide, lay to the east and south-east of the house. A two-storey 18th century Dove-House, standing 20 feet square, lay at the north end of the west range. On the south side of the yard was a stone barn, 70 feet by 25 feet. This dated from c1800, being re-roofed in the early 20th century.

Blackbird Leys Farm viewed from the top of Evenlode Tower, at the bottom of Windale Avenue. This splendid avenue was probably laid out by the Morrell family. Only the southern portion of Windale now remains, but a few trees remain within the carpark of the Blackbird Leys Leisure Centre, indicating the original extended line of the avenue. The farm remained after the development of the Estate, and was a favorite route for cross-country runs from the local schools.

Windale Avenue in 1992 and the gates which stood at the entrance to the farm. The barn, which still stands as part of the new development, can be seen at the end of the avenue.

A Roman road, sixteen miles long, has always formed the eastern boundary of Sandford parish. This major north-south route linked two minor Roman towns, Alchester (to the north near Bicester) and Dorchester-on-Thames to the south. The Road was recognised as the estate boundary in Anglo-Saxon times and was referred to as 'thaere Straet', or 'the Street'. In 1820 the Road was named as 'Blackbridge Lane' and was included within Blackbridge Leaze Farm, as Blackbird Leys Farm was then called (Oxford City Archives K/37/2b-c). Later in the 19th century it was referred to as 'Blackber's Lane'.

At some time in the 16th century the small tenant-farmers of Sandford parish, exchanged and consolitated their many widely-scattered and mixed strips of arable land in the Open Fields. This created larger and more convenient fields from blocks of strips. Several groups of fields in the south and east of the parish were taken out of the normal pattern of arable and fallow in the Open Fields and became 'Leys' — land used as pasture or arable as circumstances dictated. Knapps Leys lay in the south of the Sandford parish, Goulds, or Golden, Leys in the middle, Fursey Leys, now known as Sandford Brake Farm, in the south-east corner and Black-Ford Leys in the north-east corner. Farms were built on some of these Leys — one of them being Blackford, later Blackbird, Leys, Farm.

North of Blackbird Leys Farmhouse, a stream flows west in a channel that may have been man-made, perhaps to clear the land for farming in the 9th or 10th centuries. This stream was known as Black Brook; now known as Northbrook Stream. Blackbird Leys Estate was developed on the site of Sawpit Farm, in the parish of Littlemore, but taking its poetic name from Blackbird Leys Farm, in the neighbouring parish of Sandford.

This council housing estate to the south east of Oxford, was built in the 1960s. With the growth of the nearby car industry homes were required for additional factory workers. The City Council planned to build an estate of 2800 dwellings on land used by the sewage works and Sawpit Farm, and outline planning permission was granted in 1953. The farmland belonging to Blackbird Leys Farm was owned by the City of Oxford from 1895 and was brought within the City boundary in April 1991. (Based on The History, Landscape and Buildings of Blackbird Leys Farm, Oxford, by David Sturdy, a survey for Ealing Family Housing Association.)

'The field known as Spring Piece was one of the fields which used to flood from time to time, converted into a black, evil smelling bog which encouraged flies and mosquitos in their thousands. Other parts of the sewage farm were dug by hand into gridiron shapes known locally as the beds and on these, that is the raised or banked portion, was grown such crops as mangolds, cabbages and Brussel sprouts, which needed very little further encouragement to grow. As youngsters we would search for the nests and eggs of the lapwing or pee-wit, leaping from quaking bog to quaking bog, often as not getting a shoeful of the vile muck as a reward for our pains. Looking at the fields one day, when the first faint murmurings of building on them began to be heard, the wiseacres of the locality shook their heads and said, with what emphasis they could muster, "they'll never build on them", but they did, as witness the Evenlode and Windrush Towers standing there now.' (Memories of George Bampton of Littlemore)

An area of 260 acres was set aside for the new estate. The main road into this new estate was along Long Lane in Littlemore, crossing the railway line over a small hump-backed bridge – known as Morrells Bridge. This photograph of 1958 shows the progress of the Eastern By-Pass, with Barns Road across the middle. The railway line runs across the bottom, just above the tree-lined Sandy Lane. Long Lane is on the left hand side and the position of the railway bridge can be pin-pointed. The Stadium is at the bottom on the extreme right, with greyhound kennels to the side.

Development

An aerial photograph taken in April 1961.

Morrells bridge crosses the railway line on the left hand side. This was the only entrance to the Estate, apart from the Watlington Road/Sandy Lane end. Excavations are taking place for the Blackbird Leys flyover, to eventually join the Airfield Estate along Barns Road. Sandy Lane, joining the Watlington Road at the top, follows the original line of this road, with the distinctive bend on the left hand side, just below the Stadium. On the Blackbird Leys side of Morrells bridge was a property called The Bungalow, occupied by Ross Druce, who gave his name to Druce Way. Blackbird Leys County Primary School can be seen at the top right, beyond which lay fields. *'Public transport was not very reliable. Kent Close was the terminus and a bus was supposed to run every 35 minutes, but this could not be relied upon. A more reliable bus service was the Watlington bus along the other end of Sandy Lane.'* Fox

Sawpit Cottages

Mrs Deadman in front of No 2 Sawpit Cottages, which used to be situated in the area of present-day Evenlode Tower. No 2 was previously occupied by the Quarterman family, when Mr Quarterman was a foreman at the Sewage Works. The next door cottage, No 1, was occupied by the Taylor family. The sewage farm can be seen on the left of this photograph, opposite the lane. *'Pheasants flew everywhere, with chickens, pigeons, rabbits and moorhens. We shopped at Rose Hill, and at Mrs Harvey's little shop in Spring Lane. The cottages had no electric and no gas, just paraffin lamps and a big black leaded kitchen range for heating.'*

The Deadman family moved on 8 August 1961, at which time building was taking place adjacent to the cottages.

The first houses occupied on Blackbird Leys were numbers 23-33 Sandy Lane, seen here in August 1958, looking west towards what was to become Furlong Close. The first residents were Edward Wall (no 23), Andrew Murphy (no 25), Albert Green (no 27), Albert Collier (no 29), John Green (no 31) and Ron Chandler (no 33). A stream originally ran in front of these houses and caused flooding to the front gardens. Railway sleepers had to be laid across the stream before residents could move in. It was eventually diverted to a concrete culvert on the opposite side of the road. The stream ran from the Scout Hut in Sandy Lane through to the allotments off Kestrel Crescent.

By September 1958, ten families with children were living on the embryo Estate. These families, seen here in Sandy Lane, were among a number of Blackbird Leys parents who were protesting at having to walk their children one-and-a-half miles to Rose Hill School while transport was still being sorted out. Left to right: -, Mrs Green, Pauline Green, Paul Green, Valerie Green, Marion Bromley, Nigel Bromley, Mrs Bromley.

In this 1961 view the greyhound stadium can be seen at the top on the right hand side, with the railway marking the top boundary. On the right hand side, standing isolated, is the original church hut, with the school playing fields behind. Windrush Tower and Blackbird Leys Road are under construction and Knights Road is being developed. The building at the bottom, in Knights Road, is Northfield House old people's home. Knights Road was originally known as Ladenham Road, when it was no more than a dirt track leading across the fields. Its name is taken from Knights Piece, the area of land at the end of the present day Knights Road.

Sandy Lane Recreation Ground on the right hand side. The rectangular padding pool was originally part of South Eastern pumping station for sewage filtration, and can be identified in the photograph on page 14. Unfortunately, over the years the pool area was damaged and the pool has now been filled in.

Early on Sunday 5 November 1961 the old railway bridge in Long Lane was demolished. The bridge, over 100 years old, was unusual in that it had a free-standing arch, not sitting on any abutment. Nearly 200 gelignite charges were used, and the fire brigade stood by. *'Residents were warned beforehand, but were still shocked by the massive explosion. Every window on the estate must have rattled, as a large dust cloud rose into the sky.'*

Windrush Tower on the corner of Blackbird Leys Road and Knights Road, nearing completion in 1961.

The builders John Laing & Son Limited, marked each floor with the date of completion. Blackbird Leys Road is at the bottom, with Knights Road under construction on the left hand side and Merlin Road on the right. The land to the right of Windrush Tower, opposite the health centre, was once vast lagoons, built up with massive grassed banks, part of the sewage farm.

A second tower block, Evenlode Tower, was started in 1962 at the far end of Blackbird Leys Road, facing Pegasus Road. These were both 15 storey tower blocks each containing fifty-eight, two-bedroom flats and two one-bedroom flats. Each Tower Block was 150 ft high, laundry and drying space was provided on the roof, screened by a 4ft high parapet wall.

Windrush Tower was opened by the Mayor of Oxford, Alderman Lionel Harrison, on 9 April 1962. The building in the foreground is the parade of shops on Blackbird Leys Road.

Families were moved onto the new estate from all over Oxford and beyond. Many came from the Slade, an area of nissen huts lying between Cowley and Headington, which were used during the second world war and later housed families of men working at Morris's factory. Rehousing also took place from St Ebbe's in Oxford centre, which was being completely demolished. The houses on Blackbird Leys were very modern and were the height of luxury when compared to the older dilapidated housing that had been left behind.

During the first stages of development, houses in Sandy Lane and Kent Close, semi-detached with a garage attached, were built by Laings. The ones built on the opposite side of Sandy Lane were a different design, with the kitchens facing the main road, but these did not prove very popular with residents.

Further development took place in Tucker Road, Sawpit Road, Blay Close and Wesley Close. Balfour Road was developed, which allowed for gradual infilling of Ladenham, Wingate Close and Moorbank. These last three areas had been planned to allow maximum play areas for children by forming cul-de-sacs with green turf and footpaths. At this time all the housing had open fires and the design of these cul-de-sacs were not popular with tradespeople, particularly coal deliveries.

The estate was gradually developed from one area to another, moving in an anti-clockwise direction, finishing with the Druce Way area with a much higher density than had been the original intention for the estate. (Fox)

Health Service

Sandy Lane in 1967.

Dr David Thomas, and his wife Jill and family, moved to Blackbird Leys in early 1961. They were seeking a property large enough to house their growing family, they eventually had seven children, and found the above property, then known as The Firs, which belonged to the Oxford Greyhound Stadium. They moved in and renamed the house White Buffalo. The property had extensive grounds, including a pond, a pool and tennis courts. White Buffalo became the local health surgery for the early residents, with a ground floor room serving as a surgery. Dr Thomas covered all of Garsington, as well as Blackbird Leys, and people used to sit on the stairs while waiting to see him. Early residents may remember a large statue in the hall — often referred to as the doctor's rude statue. Dr Thomas was often seen striding round the estate, with his glasses on top of his head, his stethoscope around his neck, and his faithful black labrador, Mellie, following. Dr Thomas moved from White Buffalo to Boars Hill during the 1980s, but maintained his practise until his death on 17 February 1989. The property was re-purchased by the Stadium, the house demolished and the site developed.

A house in Balfour Road was allocated to the Heath Visitors, Miss Tattersall occupying the flat upstairs and the downstairs being used for baby clinics and the purchase of powdered milk and orange juice.

The Church

The original church hut, facing the newly built Blackbird Leys Road at the bottom right, with school playing fields behind and the first buildings of Redefield School at the top. Note the original lane in front of the hut which lead to Windale Avenue. There is, of course, no sign of Cuddesdon Way.

The first Priest-Missioner, Peter Malton (1960-65) moved with his wife, Ann, and baby son, from Hammersmith in West London, into 17 Blackbird Leys Road on 21 June 1960. The first service was held in his front room on St Peter's Day, 29 June, with two communicants. In those first few months baptisms were often held in the people's own houses, and the Children's Service soon outgrew the Malton's house and moved into the newly built Health Centre, also in use by the Roman Catholic congregation. By Christmas 1960 the Diocese had provided a wooden Hut, originally situated on the Blackbird Leys Road side of the present church site, and the first service there was Midnight Communion with 16 communicants.

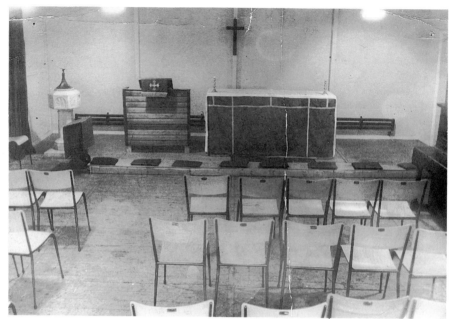

The interior of the church hut. One end of the hut, with the Altar, was curtained off so that the rest could be used for weekday activities. The Hut was the centre of all early social activities: the community centre was only opened in January 1964. The hut became the focal point for many groups, including scouts, guides, brownies, tap-dancing, junior and senior youth clubs, band practice, table tennis and the Co-Op Guild. Socials were held there and it also acted as a changing room for the local football club.

The newly positioned church hut, with the finished vicarage behind.

In August 1963 it was necessary to move the church hut, as it was exactly where the main entrance to the new church building would be. Members of the Youth Club offered to move the hut to the opposite end of the church site, facing onto the now finished Cuddesdon Way. At this time the hut was in a bad state of repair and moving it didn't help. Church services continued, despite no electricity and a leaky roof. Peter Malton himself turned labourer and finished putting in the necessary drains.

In the summer of 1981 the old church hut was in danger of falling down, and a permanent hall would soon be required. The ceremony of cutting the first turf for the new hall was carried out in 1982 by one of the youngest members, four year old Theo Addae, and one of the oldest members, the pianist at the time, Mr Ted Anderson. The second turf was cut by Rev. Tony Williamson in his capacity as Mayor of Oxford.

In September 1961 a Working Party had been formed to work on plans for a new church building. This committee, three men and one woman, comprised Jack Argent churchwarden, Charlie Brown, Roland Minchin and Betty Moss, daughter of Alice Moss. The building was designed by architect, Colin Shewring who produced a model of the proposed new building in December 1961. Peter Malton worked tirelessly to raise funds for the new church, and building finally commenced in the Spring of 1964. The foundations were laid in April 1964 and that August the Altar Stone was dedicated and then covered up as the shell of the building was built over and round it. By the time it was finished Peter Malton, the first Priest-Missioner, had left and was succeeded by Mervyn Pulleston (1965-70) who, together with his wife, Carole, moved into the newly-built Church House in Cuddesdon Way on 15 January 1965. The new church was dedicated by the Bishop of Oxford on the eve of Palm Sunday, 10 April 1965. In 1962, a Free Church Council had been formed, and Blackbird Leys was declared an 'area of ecumenical sharing'. In September of the next year, a Congregational Minister, Barry Jones (1965-72) was appointed and held the first Free Church service in the new church in October 1965.

Barry Jones left in 1972, and the Free Church staff place was kept open by Sylvia Barnes. In July 1973 agreement was reached for the appointment of a Free Church Minister jointly funded by the Baptist, Methodist and United Reformed Church and David Rowland (1974-85) was appointed in March 1974.

Audrey and David Rowland, with son Ian, after a week-long 300 hundred mile sponsored cycle ride in May 1982, which raised over £1,000 towards the new church hall.

The new hall and extension was finished in September 1983, and the old church hut was finally demolished. It comprised a hall, kitchen, multi-purpose space, and offices. It was used as the base of a weekday Neighbourhood Centre, part of the Oxford Good Neighbour Scheme, and also used by the City Council Housing Department and the County Council Social Services Department.

September 1983, upon completion of the new hall. Ian Rowlands on the right, youngest son of David and Audrey Rowlands. Jack Argent churchwarden is holding the cross.

Stephen Heap succeeded David Rowland as Free Church Minister, inducted on 16 February 1986. Stephen and his wife, Liz, settled into the Manse at 58 Blackbird Leys Road. Stephen is seen here behind Ian Clamp holding the cross.

On the Anglican side, John Strong was a worker-priest at Cowley who was also attached to Holy Family Church (1964-67). When Mervyn Pulleston left for Kidlington, he was succeeded by Tony Moore (1970-81). He was succeeded by Priest-Missioner, Michael Doe (1981-87), and currently by James Ramsay.

20th anniversary of the church

On 29 June 1980 to celebrate the first church service held on the estate, a large company, including the uniformed organisations, assembled outside 17 Blackbird Leys Road, the home of Peter Malton, the first Priest-Missioner. The service was conducted by Mark Boon, Rev. Tony Moore and Rev. David Rowland. This group includes, from the front to the back, Patsy Spencer, Janet Whitman, Susie Moore, Karen Lawson, Dorian Murphy, Mrs Pau, Hazel Moore, Angela Brown, Nancy Edwards, and Val Dillon.

The group then proceeded to the Health Centre, a reminder of the time when the congregation used the health centre building for services, then on to the church. A picnic was held afterwards, on the grass between the old church hut and the church. Seen here passing the community centre on Blackbird Leys Road, this group includes from left to right: Val Dillon, Angela Brown, Ruth Edwards, Caroline Dillon, Dorian Murphy, Hazel Moore, Rachel Berry.

To celebrate the 25th anniversary of the church in 1985, church leaders and worshippers, formed the figure 25 on the grass outside the church.

SKETCH PLAN ONLY

Development in 1964 included the building of the Pegasus Road and Field Avenue areas. Pegasus commemorates the famous Pegasus Football team and the emblem of the Knights Templar at nearby Minchery Farm. The small roads leading off Field Avenue were named alphabetically, hence Andromeda Close at one end and Woodruff Close at the other. An area of some 14 acres was left as recreation ground between Pegasus Road and Cuddesdon Way. This included two enclosed play areas for younger children, a bowling green and pavilion, football pitches and car parking space.

Community Development

Audrey Rowlands, standing on the left, at the Neighbourhood Centre c1985.

Good Neighbour Scheme

Audrey Rowland initiated a Good Neighbour Scheme, a voluntary scheme designed to offer help with transport for hospital appointments, shopping and visiting. In 1978 it made use of the front entrance and a small back room at the church on one day a week for a Friendship and Information Centre. This formed the origins of the Neighbourhood Centre. After eighteen months the Centre was open for five days a week and became an important hub in the development of the estate. In 1983, when the new part of the church building was opened, the Neighbourhood Centre moved into these larger premises. A coffee bar was open every day and the Centre operated an information desk staffed by trained workers to advise on social and welfare rights.

The Inaugural Meeting of the Neighbourhood Council was held on 18 November 1980, at which time Jack Argent was elected chairman. Daniel Inness was vice-chairman, with the Rev Tony Moore Treasurer, Andrew McLuskey Secretary and Bryan Gomm Press Officer. The estate was divided into fourteen wards, with two representatives from each ward.

Jack Argent and his wife, Iris, moved to Peregrine Road in the 1960s and immediately became deeply involved in community life. Amongst other things, he was chairman of the Blackbird Leys community centre and a founder member and church warden at the Holy Family Church. He was also chairman of the neighbourhood council and belonged to the Federation of Community Associations. He was a well-known sight on his bicycle and a greatly respected community leader within Blackbird Leys. Following his death in March 1990, at the age of 73, a memorial bench, known as the Jack Argent Seat, was placed on the green in front of the Blackbird Leys Road shops, but this was later moved to a position in front of the council offices in Cuddesdon Way.

Anne Bartlett on the left and Ann Evans on the right, volunteer helpers at the Neighbourhood Council

The Neighbourhood Council was dissolved in 1991 when Blackbird Leys became a parish with its own Parish Council, but most of the representatives remained in office. Amongst many other duties, a sub-committee of the Neighbourhood Council, originally comprising Carol Grant, Sheila Roberts, Eileen Clements and Danny Inness, produced the first issues of the Blackbird Leys Newsletter.

Through the Neighbourhood Council a Savings Club, for the benefit of residents, was started in 1989, which developed into a Credit Union. A Tenants and Residents Association was started in February 1989, formed in response to the 1988 Housing Act to represent the interests of all those living on the estate, regarding their housing and environment. Their initial chairman was Mr George Legge.

Blackbird Leys Festival

The Dressed Pram parade along Blackbird Leys Road, at the junction with Moorbank, in June 1965. The health centre on the left side side was originally built to include a large area, with a grilled entrance, where parents could leave their prams and push-chairs. The centre has recently been completely re-built.

The winners of the Soap Box Derby in the 1965 Festival. Michael Hall, is on the left holding the cup, with driver Clive Harding at the bottom of the photograph.

Derek Frith, Community Centre warden, and Dan Dunton, assistant warden, were both involved in arranging the first nine-day festival in July 1964. Activities included a children's art show, with first prize going to Sally Willetts, go karting, beauty demonstrations, weight lifting, and culminating in a day-long fete and bar-b-que. The festival later became a week-long event, the highlight of which was a parade through the estate, with decorated floats representing almost every organisation within the estate, from scouts, guides and brownies, to the community association and senior citizens' luncheon club.

Michael and Patrick Maloney about to pass Michael Hall and Trevor Reason in the Soap Box Derby at the Blackbird Leys Festival in August 1966.

Fancy Dress competitors at the Festival in 1968.

Members of the Senior Citizens bingo club from Northbrook House in Knights Road, at the Festival in June 1968.

The Rev. David Rowland was instrumental in reviving the annual Festival in 1975, but by the late 1980s the organisation of such a large event was left to just a few individuals and a week of activities was no longer possible. In 1992 the leading organisers were Ian Clamp and Jim Hewitt, with a supporting committee.

Participants in the Festival during the 1980s, include two well known characters on the estate, Elsie Poulton and Alice Moss, seated in the left of the carriage.

Members of Blackbird Leys Saturday School in the late 1980s.

Walkers from Wesley Green school taking part in the 1991 Festival. Representatives from every organisation took part and paraded through the streets of the estate.

Brownies, Guides and Scouts

The 1st Blackbird Leys Brownies added their own touch of sunshine to the Festival procession as marching majorettes, in June 1989, *'the hottest Saturday this year. Brightly decorated vehicles were judged by the Sheriff of Oxford Betty Standingford, before they paraded through the streets of Blackbird Leys to Pegasus School, where the Festival Fete was being held in the school grounds. Winners of the first prize for best festival float were the Merlin Road Family Centre who created a float with a circus theme.'* Left to right front row: Stacey Speakman, Samantha Speakman, Hayley Whitman, Angela-, Kerry-. Second row: -, Sally Wickens, Emily Manning, Kelly-, Sasha Mullee. Back includes: Kelly Pargeter, Nicola Lockyer.

The 1st Brownies at the 1992 festival, at which time the judging was held within the car park of the Leisure Centre on Pegasus Road. This group includes, standing: Emily Walker, Samantha O'Connor, Emily Manning, Christina-, Katrina Mazey. Seated: Melanie Regan, Hayley Winstone, Aimee Pargeter, Louise Newbigging, Sarah Clarke, Ellena Prescott, Gemma Howard, Yolanda Mitchell, Hannah Howard, Melissa Caan, Laura Brown. The group leaders at the back are: Mavis Harris, Christine Walker, Gillian Manning, Nancy Edwards.

The 2nd Oxford (Blackbird Leys) Boys' Brigade was formed in 1966. The photograph, taken in April 1967, shows the new colours which had presented to the company's captain, Mr David Cowan, by Mrs Eleanor Davis. The colours had been dedicated by the Rev. Mervyn Puleston, at a service conducted by the Rev. Barry Jones, Free Church chaplain. The materials for the colours were paid for by the St Columba's Presbyterian Church, Oxford and the colours were made by Mrs Helen Cowan, wife of the company's captain. The tall boy behind the flag is Brian Coombes, Francis Summersbee, Edmund Strzlecki, Martin Long and Henry O'Connor are also included.

The uniformed youth of Blackbird Leys, outside the Church of the Sacred Heart in Sawpit Road, assembling for another street parade during Festival Week.

Co-operative Women's Guild

The Blackbird Leys branch of the Co-operative Women's Guild was formed in 1976. Seen here at the 1983 Festival, dressed as St Trinian School Girls, left to right: Elsie Poulton, Daphne Lamb, Alice Lennon, Bette Stone, Jean Peach, Mavis Harris, Audrey John, Eileen-, Jacky Gunnett.

Members of the Guild met for a photograph early in the morning outside the church of The Sacred Heart, on the corner of Balfour and Sawpit Roads, to celebrate Elsie Poulton's 80th birthday. Left to right: Mavis Harris, Brenda Hunter, Alice Moss, Alice Lennon, Elsie Poulton, Jacky Gunnett, Daphne Lamb, Audrey John, Heather Cook. Elsie lived at 91 Balfour Road and was very well known on the Estate.

The Community Association

The first Annual General Meeting of the Community Association was held in February 1963, at which Peter Malton was elected Secretary and Jack Argent chairman, a post he held until his death in 1990. Jack Argent on the left, with Peter Malton on the right.

Saturday Cinema Show in March 1964. Mervyn Puleston on left and Francis Spiers, treasurer of the Community Association.

Mervyn Puleston became Secretary of the Community Association upon his appointment, and his wife Carole came onto the committee, and was later Assistant Warden until 1971. Mrs Puleston, with a few other mums from the estate, started a Saturday morning picture show, known as KKK or Kiddies Kinema Klub. This was originally intended for children between the ages of 5 and 9, but developed into a Cinema Club for older children and teenagers. Mr Derek Frith had been appointed full time Warden of the Association, and is well remembered by those attending the Club; he was able to gain absolute silence merely by standing on the stage!

The Community Association was responsible for introducing Qualidays — a new word for the English language. Qualidays, held four times a year, aimed to give senior citizens on the estate a *'taste of the good life'*, with lunch and entertainment. The Lonely and Disabled Club operated from the Community Centre, members of which are seen here in 1973 receiving a new club van presented by Councillor Ann Spokes Symonds kneeling in the middle of the photograph. The lady on the left, leaning on walking sticks, was Rosie Drake who lived in Moorbank, a leading light and a great worker for the Club.

The youth wing of the Community Centre was an important meeting place for the young people on the estate. Seen here are 15 year old Anita Reason on the left with 14 year old Julie Cross, probably taken in the early 1970s.

A '1972 Committee' was set up in the 1960s to look at amenities for teenagers. It was realised that by 1972 the estate would have a large number of young people, for whom provision would need to be made. Apart from the uniformed groups and youth clubs there was little else to appeal to this age group. People actively involved in youth work in the early years included Joe Williamson, Bryan Gomm, Norman Smith and Alex Dunsmuir.

The Blackbird Leys Social Club Aunt Sally 'A' team after losing the final of the Team Knock Out Cup in 1999 season. Left to right back row: Phil Hounslow, Malcolm Crook, Billy Trinder, Willy Waite, John Bailey, Phil Butler. Front row: Mick Kavanagh, Steve Tooke, Roger Goodall, Andy Beal.

The Aunt Sally 'B' team after winning Section 7 of the Morrells Summer League 1999. Left to right back row: Cliff Hornblow, Terry Beal, Clive Proudfoot, Bonner Waite, Dave Goatley. Front row: Steve Buckle, Craig Beal, Kim Proudfoot.

Jubilee Hall

At the time of the Queen's Silver Jubilee in 1977, many street parties were arranged. Local residents in the vicinity of Juniper Drive, formed the Jubilee '77 Association and the resultant celebrations were such a success they were repeated the following year, with a bumper tea party for more than 80 local children. Jubilee Hall, in Sorrell Road was built and continues to thrive in this part of the estate.

Jubilee '77 Association encouraged local children to help clear the streets of litter, seen here in 1979.

Barbara Gatehouse moved to 17 Sawpit Road Blackbird Leys from Florence Park in August 1959. Already a member of the Labour Party, Barbara became Secretary of the local branch and eventually stood for Council. She represented Blackbird Leys on the City Council from 1979 to 1996, retiring at the age of 70. Barbara was involved in many Council Committee's, including Chairing of the Recreation and Amenities Committee, and active involvement in the economic planning of the area during the closure of the Cowley Works. Barbara was Sheriff of Oxford 1990/91 and Mayor 1992/93.

Blackbird Leys can be justly proud of its local councillors, both at parish level and above. Amongst these people are included, left to right: Eileen Clements, Molly Florey, Andrew Smith, Val Smith and Carol Roberts.

This year Eileen Clements completes thirty years service with the Neighbourhood and Parish Councils. She has also been a long-serving Governor of Orchard Meadow School, and was instrumental in setting up the BMX track within Spindleberry Park. Molly Florey also started on the Neighbourhood Council and is currently chair of the Parish Council. Molly is involved in the CDI Youth Management Committee and chairs the board of Leys News. A past governor of St John Fisher School, she has given many years service to the estate. Carol Roberts, Lord Mayor of Oxford 1997-8, served on the original committee for the Adventure Playground. She also worked in the Tutorial Unit of Ivanhoe School and later Wesley Green School.

BLACKBIRD LEYS ROAD,

Littlemore.
From Long lane to 81 Pegasus road. Map I 11.

North side.

1 Goodgam D
3 Ryan T
5 Jacobs E
7 Hilsdon T
9 Piercy A. P
11 Gerken I
13 Jordan O
15 Walton F. E
17 Malton Rev. W. P. A
19 Bull B
21 Beesley W
23 Mander I
25 Bayliss A
27 Dean E
29 Saxton H. F
31 Crook L
33 Saddler A

...... here is Balfour rd ......

35 Williams R
37 Evans C
39 Louch A
41 Rowland B
43 Turnbull C
45 Irving E
47 Dillon D
49 Arnold C
51 Ackland K
53 Campbell P
55 Dean Mrs. L. A
57 Edwards T
59 Hignell F
61 Harris Saml
63 Health Centre (City of Oxford)

...... here is Moorbank ......

Blackbird P.H

... here is Cuddesdon way ...

Redefield   Secondary
Modern School (mixed)

Evenlode Tower.

1 Groundwater H. S
2 Higgs Jn
3 Clifton J. R
4 Drewitt C. H
5
6 Cook W. P
7 Evans E
8 Padwick Miss D. R
9 Walker D. H
10 Forster K. D. B
11 Jackman A. E

12
13 Howlett E. J
14 Readman J. A
15 Williams M. E
16 Ryman J. M
17 Taylor B
18 Haselden A
19 Lyon D. C
20 Woodley A. G. J
21 Mathews W. H
22 Beattie David C
23 Harvey Ronald W
24 Winter Kenneth S
25
26 Morley R
27 Weekes L. G. J
28 Nurden A. J
29 Aldsworth D. A
30 Boyce K
31 Bryant E. O
32 Bennett F. J
33 Roberts P. C
34 Lygo R. A
35 Franks R. H
36 O'Neill B. E
37 Beaver E. T
38 Cordell B. A
39 Franklin P. A
40 Hurn F. H
41 Keefe R. H
42 Taylor E. N
43 Elderfield S
44 Troth W. G. A
45 Gill W. D
46 Wilkins D. E
47 Stoder B. B
48 Sorbie W
49 Saxton E. A
50 Newell D. M
51 Clarke R. W. D
52 Tolly C. C
53 Potter R. L
54 Moran T. D
55 Wilkes P
56 Fewtnell L. H
57 Gibson N
58 Sudnay T. L
59 Harper P. T
60 Wheatley B. K

South side.

...... here is Moor bank ...

24 Gray B. A
26 Nicholls K
28 Bonney C. R
30 Ashmore F. S
32 Cook E. G
34 Coggins M
36 Wheeler G. C
38 Barson J. H
40 Butler H
42 Sawyer R. T
44 Mathews W. J
46 Lyons J

48 McGee W
50
52

...... here is Merlin rd ......

54 Roberts J
56 Gillett E
58 Best S
60 Swain R
62 Johnson G
64 Callan W
66 Peck Mrs. V
68 Holmes D
70 Holloway W. H
72 Mason G
80 Falconer Jas
100 Falconer Jas. chemist.
Tel. No. Oxford 78729
136 Gardner W. C
138 Gordon I. T
140 Brown S
142 Paddick A. O
144 Whatley P. W
146 Tweedie R. E
148 White M
150 Boyd E. K
152 Collcutt R. B
154 Whitton N
156 Caffyn T
158 Bridgewater H
160 Loughran E. O
162 Shorter J

MONKS CLOSE.

From Merlin road.
(No thoroughfare.)
North side.

21 Marvin Mrs. G. V
20 Pullen Albt
19 Wilkins Ernest V
18 Lane Fredk
17 Chamberlain Kenneth
16 McKairne J
15 Shepherd E
14 Howell Mrs. E. E
South side.
1 Saddler G
2 Gammon Gordon
3 Newman Mrs. P
4 Robinson J
5 Grant Mrs
6 Halton V
7 Evett Arth
8 Hastings Mrs
9 Rowlands Frank
10 Evans Oswald
11 Brough Roy
12 Dandridge G
13 Hunter G

FIELD AVENUE.

From Pegasus avenue.
Map I 11 & J 11.

South side.

2 Strange K. G
4 Cimmernanis H
6 McCreedy C
8 Walton L. J
10 Browne G
12 Allmond T

... here are Angelica close, Bulrush road & Clover place ...

14 Bowler K
16 Thomas B
18 Montagu H. W
20 Whitman M. H
22 Burrage M
24 Pitts Mrs. S. M
26 Watkins C. R
28 Devonport H. E
30 Collyer G. F

...... here are Flaxfield & Gentian roads ......

32 Lowe N. J
34 Davies R. F
36 Constance C. R
38 Musto B. A
40 Miller B. R
42 Grant P
44 Kinsella M
46 Fryer J. E

...... here is Lobelia rd .....

KESTREL PLACE.

(Formerly Kestrel close.)
From 132 Kestrel crescent.
Map H 11.
(No thoroughfare.)

South-east side.

1 Richardson S
2 McDonald E. J
3 Norris A. E
4 Butcher H
5 Page Mrs. P
6 Bujko Mrs. G
7 Collett Mrs. M
8 Elliott J

North-west side.

9 Tackley D
10 Brown O
11 Bingham K
12 Lawson A
13 Lee B

Extracts from Kellys Directory, 1964 (by kind permission of Reed Information Systems).

Schooling

The original teachers at Blackbird Leys County Primary School, 1959. Left to right back row: Cecil Jacobs, Mrs Nicholls, David Munday, Robin Cox. Front row: Miss Fazakerley, Miss Martin, Miss Macdiarmid.

Families with young children flooded the new estate, and a school was built in Wesley Close. This opened on 14 September 1959 with a staff of six, under the headship of Mr Cecil Jacobs, and with 94 children, mixed infants and juniors.

'Less than a decade ago Blackbird Leys was wild open countryside with not a house to be seen except Blackbird Leys Farm nestling at the bottom of the tall elms in the middle of the fields. During the late fifties development began and with it the first foundations of our school were laid in 1958. By September 1959 the school was ready to receive its first pupils and on 14 September 1959, 94 children walked rather timidly through the main gates. It was a glorious late summer day it had been the loveliest summer for many years) and the staff and children alike had the feeling of embarking on a new adventure. The school buildings were far from ready, and only five classrooms were in use, three infant and two junior. There was no staff room, hall, canteen (a classroom was used) or headmaster's room and for the first term we had to make do as well as we could. Little did we realise at the time that it was to be nearly four and a half years before all the building was complete.' Peel

Blackbird Leys County Primary School nearing completion in 1959. This photograph was taken at the 'cross-roads' of several original farm tracks, before the playing fields were laid. The lane to the left lead to the Lodge, near the old Morrells Bridge, to the right to Sawpit Cottage, straight ahead to Garsington and back along the line of present-day Knights Road. Houses on the left, the back of Blay Close, and on the right, Sawpit Road, are under construction.

Miss Martin's Class Nativity Play in 1959. These children would have been some of the first ninety-four children to join the school on the day of opening, 14 September 1959.

An after-school club was organised in 1960 by teacher, Gordon Peel, running twice a week from 4.00 to 6.00 p.m. This offered activities for 7-11 year olds, catering for the 150 children in this age group who lived on the estate at this time. Mr Peel ran football training for the boys, while Miss Pauline Whittaker ran PE classes and country dancing, Miss Margaret Macdiarmiad, seen above, supervised the art and craft room and Mr David Munday the indoor games room.

Children were admitted to the school every week and by the autumn of 1960 there were 283 children and eight teachers. Average numbers in each of the lower classes were 38 to 40. Builders were always on the site as new classrooms were constructed.

Christmas 1960 and Class J2, the cast of the production 'Who will hold the Giant?'. Left to right back row: Nigel Morris, -, -, -, Gillian Aspel. Middle row: Christine Gniady, -, Marilynne Waite, -, -, -, Marion Bromley, Beverley Chandler?. Front row: Ann Fitzgerald, Jenny Wheable, Mary and Margaret Bowers, Ellis Taylor, Carole Young, Lorraine Kinch, -, -.

The children were not allowed to ride bicycles to school until they had passed their Cycling Proficiency Tests, seen here in 1960. The children received certificates, badges and pennants. In 1960 10 children passed their Test, 10 in 1961, 62 in 1962, 45 in 1963 and 49 in 1964.

Part of the Cycling Proficiency Test in the school playground. The houses in the background, not yet completed, are numbers 2 to 8 Moorbrook, while the back of Blay Close is on the right hand side.

A Third Cycling Course was held at the school in May under the direction of Mr Wall (Road Safety Officer). Twenty children took part, giving us a total of 40 who have passed the course since the school opened. Boys: Michael Norwood, Barry Morris, Geoffrey Gamage, Peter Crook, David Cook, Ronald Godfrey, Ellis Taylor, Paul Mayell, Douglas Reason, Michael Mazurek, Michael Webster, Malcolm Harris. Girls: Valerie Walters, Teresa McCann, Linda Drewitt, Susan Beasley, Janis Drewitt. School Magazine 1962.

School football teams 1960/61. Left to right back row: Rodney Newbold, Michael Webster, Stephen Long, Gordon Peel teacher, -, Charles Unwin, Barry Tyas, -. Middle row: Malcolm Harris, Stephen Holloway, Colin Easterbrook, Terry Waite, Mickie Mazurek, Alan Norwood, Michael Partlett. In front: -, Ian Pullen, Peter Zimmer.

Athletics group, September 1961. Left to right back row: Rosemary Marshall teacher, Michael Webster, -, Alan Howells?, Malcolm Harris, Michael Mazurek, Barry Tyas, Terry Waite, Alan Norwood, Gordon Peel teacher. Seated: Hazel Zimmer, Pauline Tolley, Dorothy Smith, Angela Stratton, Gwyneth Long, -, Sandra Harris, Carol Gossen, Angela Cooke. In front: Brian Cook, -.

Top class in 1961. Left to right back row: David Munday teacher, Derek Patterson?, -, -, -, Barry Tyas, -, Mick Partlett, -, -, Terry Waite, Charles Unwin, Peter Zimmer, Jimmy McCairns?, Ian Pullen, -, -, Cecil Jacobs headmaster. Middle row seated: Pauline Tolley, -, -, -, Gwyneth Long, Carol Gossen, -, Jenny Beale?, -, Sandra Harris, -. Front row: -, -, -, Irene Cooke, -, -, Christine Allen?, -, Margaret Newman, -, -, Rodney Newbold?.

Class J4A at Christmas 1962. Left to right back row: -, Linda Mysliewiez, Alison Handley, -, Lesley Godfrey, Gillian Aspel, -, Jenny Wheable, Pat Young, Nigel Morris. Next row: Pauline Buckwell, -, Janice Deacon, Alan Williams, Barbara Cook, Peter Fowler, -, -. Next row: Robert Hilsdon, Suzanne State, -, Carole Young, -, Christine Gniady, Stephen Long, Janis Drewett, Charles Unwin, Pat Haynes. In front: John Beale, Barry Harris, -, Robert Dean, -.

Roller skating competitions held in the playground in 1960, watched by Mrs Nicholls on the right hand side. *Once again a most interesting roller skating championship was held at Easter. After some thrilling races and a few spills the winners emerged as follows: 1st year boys: John Cooper, girls: Moira Gibbons. 2nd year boys: Nicholas Burden, girls: Elaine Cartwright. 3rd year boys: Peter Fowler, girls: Barbara Cook. 4th year boys: Barry Jones, girls: no competition.* School Magazine 1962

Members of the school Cycling Club in June 1961. Left to right: Alan Norwood, C Grace, S McGuire, Michael Partlett, Graham Weatherby, Derek Paterson.

School visit to Buckingham Palace Mews and the Science Museum in 1962. Left to right: Christine Allen, Gillian Aspel, Carole Young, Lorraine Chamberlain, Barbara Cook, Irene Cooke, Janis Drewitt, Maureen Cooper, Valerie Walters, Sheila Winston, Penny Beat.

Blackbird Leys Infant School opened on 29 March 1961 under the headship of Miss Pam Drury. At this time the main school had 332 children and was bursting at the seams - one teacher had 51 children in her class.

'During the first year the school grew and new children were admitted every week. Our first major change came about April 1961 when the school was split into two schools and Miss Drury took five classes with her to the Infants and we were left with seven. Building continued apace and on 7 June 1962 after the piles had been sunk, four temporary buildings were erected to the south east of the school. This was a fascinating project as the cranes quickly swung whole sections into position and the classes were ready within two days.

By the start of the spring term 1962 our numbers had so increased that the hall was again used as a classroom. The third Annual Dinner was held at the end of January and over 70 people attended. The staff gave a short entertainment entitled 'Slipped Disc'. Also during this term visits were arranged to the Science Museum and Buckingham Palace Mews and the school choir took part in the Junior Schools' Festival at the Town Hall. Six-a-side football and seven-a-side netball were arranged for the first time.' Peel

School choir practising for the Junior Schools' Festival in 1962. The choir was lead by music teacher, Valerie Lucas.

The first school fete, held 7 July 1962, with Graeme and Clive Young. This fete was held to raise funds towards the new swimming pool. *In the summer term, on 7 July, after many months of preparation our first school fete was held. It was a complete success, with about 1000 people attending and receipts being over £200.* Peel

During the harsh winter of 1962/63 the playground was a complete sheet of ice. Mr Jacobs, the headmaster, instead of banning the children from the playground, organised sliding competitions - and the teachers showed how this was done!

School netball team, March 1963. Left to right: Rosemary Marshall teacher, Gillian Aspel (goal), Pat Young (shooter), Linda Mysliewiec (goal defence), Janice Deacon (centre), Pauline Buckwell (goal attack), Janis Drewett (wing attack), Linda Deacon (reserve), Linda Moxham (wing defence).

'September 1963 - the great event on the sports side this year was the winning of the Oxford Junior Schools Netball Tournament. Our girls brought back with them the first sports trophy the school had won. Peel.

At the beginning of the school's fourth year, September 1962, it was decided to have a House System in the school. Children were divided into four Houses, known at first by their colours, Red, Yellow, Blue and Green. Eventually it was decided to name them after the Patron Saints of the British Isles - St George's Red, St David's Yellow, St Andrew's Blue and St Patricks Green. Points were awarded to individuals taking part in inter-house sports, competitions, quizzes, swimming galas, and many other activities. Points were totalled fortnightly and the position of the House Banners in the Hall changed accordingly. The Banners were designed based on mythical beasts connected with the country, the emblem of the country and the flag of the Patron Saint. These were worked into a design by Miss Valerie Lucas and Mrs McNay. Christine and Caroline Gniady, Noreen Collins and Janis Drewitt were chosen to work the embroidery on felt and to stitch the shapes on to the background.

The children took part in 'standards' for running, jumping and throwing, for which Certificates were issues. In 1962 277 children took part: only 33 passed all three standards. Special mention was made of Sonia Williamson, who had passed all three standards for every year.

During the summer term, athletic standards were again set to all the children in the school according to their age. The following boys and girls gained certificates (Passed all Standards) for 1962. Boys: Charles Unwin, Paul Tackley, Stephen Gossen, Kenneth Plested, Stephen Greenaway, Paul Day, T Jones, R Finch, R Greenwood, Michael Taylor, S Green, David Orman, Clive Young, Barry Waite, Freddie Bentley, Terry Butler. Girls: Susan Beasley, Alison King, Pauline Buckwell, Lorraine Lee, Elizabeth Salter, Nanette Tombs, C Walker, Anita Green, Sonia Williamson, Faith Goodgame, Linda Kupka, C Gniady, Danuta Bednarz, Sally Willett, Desde Holland, Amanda Steele, C Evans. School Magazine

Lorraine Kinch as Princess Miranda in the school play, The Stammering Princess, in 1963. Following this production, Lorraine was chosen to sing the part of 'Tina' in the Oxford Operatic Society's production of 'The Little Sweep'. She joined the Royal Academy of Music at the age of 18, enjoying a successful career in opera and solo concerts, now a singing teacher at Milton Keynes.

The three Maids in Waiting played by Linda Mysliewiec (Lady Amelia), Barbara Cook (Lady Amanda) and Janice Deacon (Lady Amy).

Other cast members included: Robert Hilsdon as Tom, Stephen Smith as Dick, Timothy Hanks as Harry, Terrence Seeney as Oldest Inhabitant, Ellis Taylor as King of Barania, Richard Cresswell as the Page, Julia Cook, Jane Fowler, Irene Jones, Colin Evans, Lorraine Harwood, Barbara Bednartz as the Children, and Barry Harris as the Bandit.

'The highlight of the spring term 1963 was undoubtedly the production of 'The Stammering Princess' when three fine performances were given at school and one to the children at the Wingfield Hospital. December 2nd 1963 is worth mentioning for on that day the school was completely finished and handed over by the builders. This was the first time since September 1959 that we had been completely free from builders. At the beginning of the spring term 1964 there were 450 children and 13 staff. All the main building was in use, plus one of the huts.' Peel

Staff in 1965. Left to right back row: Tony Davis, Miss Edis, Nigel Simpson, Gordon Peel, Robin Cox, Cecil Jacobs headmaster, Rosemary Marshall, Jean Nicholls, David Munday. Seated: Miss Macaulay, Valerie Lucas, Robina Paley, Avril Banton, Elaine Brown, Muriel Wells, Marie Powell, Mrs Mysliewiec, Eileen Taney. In front: Sue Dykes, Cherry Barrier, Vivienne Forward.

New schools were opened to cater for the large number of children living on the estate. Overmede Infant School opened January 1965, Overmede Junior School in May 1965, both in Pegasus Road, and St John Fisher Roman Catholic School in Sandy Lane also during 1965. It was necessary to 'divide up' the estate and children living in Field Avenue and Pegasus Road area, and some of those in Knights Road and Kestrel Crescent area, were transferred to the Overmede Schools in the following May.

By 1970 both Blackbird Leys and Overmede Junior Schools were again bursting at the seams. Another primary school, to be called Ivanhoe, had been built at the end of Knights Road and the complete third year from both Blackbird Leys and Overmede Junior, staff and pupils, were transferred. This move created tension and rivalry amongst the children and it was several years before the children regained their identity.

In 1973 the three-tier system was introduced to Oxford City - First School, Middle School and Upper School, and the 11 plus exam was discontinued in Oxford. Names were changed: Blackbird Leys Infant School became Orchard Meadow, Blackbird Leys Junior School became Shepherds' Hill, Overmede Infants became Harebell School and Overmede Junior became Pegasus School. Harebell and Pegasus were later amalgamated, under the name Pegasus School, and catered for children aged from 5 to 9 years old.

Class 4a in 1964. Left to right, back row: -, -, -, Steve Gossen, -, -, -, Malcolm Weddell?, Stephen Lenhardt, -, -, -, -, -, -, Kevin Barker. Middle Row: Marian Bromley, -, Dallas Barber, Linda Deacon, Noreen Collins, Beverly Chandler, Lorraine Lee, Elizabeth Salter, -, Jane Crawford. Front row: -, Lorraine Kinch, -, Anne Cowan, Nanette Tombs, Margaret Benyon, -, Wendy Callan, Ann Taylor, -, -, -.

The girls of Class 4M Blackbird Leys School, 1971.

Staff in September 1981 'the beginning of Wesley Green'. Left to right back row: Ray Wyman, Sally Hindmarsh, Paddy Davis, Ann Burghard, Jane Jones, Phil Baum, Marlyn Scott, Evelyn Flloyd, Lesley Baxter, Anne Brewer. Next row: Kathy Kitching, Margaret Moll, Jackie Sunderland, Glyn Pryce, Roy Money, Ivor Roberts (Ivanhoe Unit), Mary Bennett, Russell Wade, supply teacher. Next row: Pam Floyd, Audrey Clark, Marilyn Street, Christine Cook, Ian Blunsdon, Heather Wilson, Shirley Bowler, Carole Roberts, Shirley Mackenzie, Jean Harwood. Front row: Margaret Peel, Joyce Hamill, Barbara Wharton, Mari Powell, Peter Roper headmaster, Hugh Turner deputy head, Gordon Peel, Sandra Cullingford, Dee Sinclair. On floor: Helena Rojinsky, Ann Makin. Mention should be made of Audrey Clark who started as school secretary in 1959, and continues to this day.

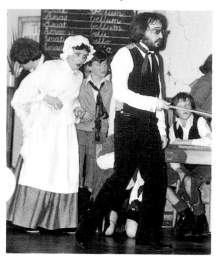

Shepherds Hill School continued the school's reputation for excellent drama productions. These included *Smike* in 1981, a pop musical freely based on Charles Dickens' *Nicholas Nickleby*. Darren Copeland took the part of 'Smike'. Teachers, Hugh Turner, playing Nicholas Nicklyby, and Margaret Peel, playing Mrs Squeers, can be seen here, with Michael Elphinstone, playing Richard, in the middle.

The Dracula Spectacular was produced in 1982. The cast included: Ann Makin as 'Miss Nadia Naive', Karen Paxford, Sharon Jones, Barbara Hunt, Peter Brown, Suzette McClean, Lisa Lewis as 'pupils'. Richard Flanagan and Thomas Flanagan as 'Airways Pilots', Amanda Burns, Carmen Harris, Rebecca Bryant, Karen Curtis, Lisa Karavias, Linda Nimmo as 'The Dynamite Dolls' and Simon Brahan as 'Genghis'.

Following the success of *The Dracula Spectacular* in 1982, Wesley Green school, as it now was called, produced *Luke Warmwater, a Star Flaws production* in 1984, a take-off of the film Star Wars. This was directed and produced by Hugh Turner, with music written by the school's head of music, Mr Ian Blunsdon. The large production involved 132 pupils: Luke Warmwater was played by Simon Brahan; Hearth Fender by Mark Marksman; RU12 by Sean Ryan; Sleepy 3-0 by Wayne St Claire; The Princess was Claire Wilson; and Sparks was Neil Hunter. Left to right front row: Susanne Wells, Wayne Sinclair, Simon Brahan, Claire Wilson, -.

Deputy head teacher, Hugh Turner, left Wesley Green Middle School at the end of the summer term in July 1985, having been deputy for the past eight years. He was appointed head teacher at Lawn Upton School in nearby Littlemore. The above photograph shows pupils celebrating the end of term with a giant picnic on the school playing fields, when Debbie Clibbon, Samantha Evans and Amelia Martin, all aged 12, won a prize for the most imaginative costumes - a trio of clowns.

Red Nose Day celebrations at Wesley Green Middle School in 1988. Left to right back row: -, Karen Cole, Stephen Lawton, Tracy Crowder, Paul Turner, Danny Brackett, Gareth Smith. Front row: Naomi Matthews, Matthew Green, -, Donna Hall, Kerry Rawlings, Emma Langton, Mrs Margaret Peel, Jane West, Vicki Harris, Lisa Stimpson, -, Stewart Caple.

Orchard Meadow Infants School

Orchard Meadow Infants School sports day probably in the late 1980s. Note the original temporary building used for Pre-School Nursery classes, with Cuddesdon Way on the right hand side.

Children from Orchard Meadow at the Sandy Lane paddling pool, in 1990, soon before its closure.

Overmede - Harebell - Pegasus Schools

Overmede School Play, possibly *Billy Budd*, taken outside the school c1968. Left to right standing: -, David Smith, Mark Ayres, -, Alex Crowe, Billy Donovan, Martin Gaisford, Kevin Roberts, Stephen Topson, Kevin Plato, Wester Welch, James Perry. Kneeling: Mark Brandon, Michael Sneade, -, Stirling Hotson, Richard Harris, Stephen Harris, -, Edward-.

Overmede school outing in 1969/70 - a cruise on the SS Nevada to Africa, Spain, Gibraltar and Portugal - at a cost of £52. Left to right: Michael Sneade, Stephen Wootton, Mr James, Stephen Hignell, Alan Bowyer, -, David Sales, Julian Howells, Phillip Bell.

Overmede school play of 1968/69. Back row: Katrina MacDonald (3rd from left), Susan Kettle (10th), Kevin Drewett (15th), Stirling Hotson (18th), Richard Harris (19th), Kevin Plato (20th), Stephen Topson (21st), Mike Sneade (22nd), Stephen Wise (end of row). Front row: Linda Barrett (2nd from left), Wendy Wise (7th from left).

Overmede Infants staff c1972. Left to right back row: -, -, Mrs Draper, Chris Freestone, Gill Mitchell, Sue Clay, Pat Linsey, -. Middle row: -, -, -, -, Pat Waller, Delia Pap, Rona Logan, Mrs Bonham. Front row: Penny-, Margaret Fryer, Mrs Martin deputy head, Audrey Parks, Miss Austin head mistress, Francis Waller, Ida Awde.

Overmede Infants class c1969. Left to right, back row: Miss Clifford, Robert Blackmore, Derek James, Tony Shaylor, -, Maureen Hudson, David McNish, Nicola Temple, -, Mark Tansley. Next row: Sylvia Welch, -, Felicity Harris, Steven Ball, Sarah Dawson, -, Deborah Smith, Joan Barrett. Next row: -, Steven Thomas, Michelle Earle, Terry Webster, Neil -, Terry Hopkins?, -, Gregor McDonald. Front row: -, Paul Clinton, Deborah Peverall, -, Teresa Carter, Christine McCarthy, Tony Hayes.

Overmede Junior School's musical production in 1971 was an operetta based on the story of Rumpelstiltskin. Teacher, Miss Archer, produced the play and eighty pupils took part in the cast, choir and orchestra. Some of the cast are seen above, left to right: Gillian Lock, Nigel Brown who played the part of Rumpelstiltskin, Wendy Wise, Paul Hackett, Madeline Dawson, Raymond Claridge.

Redefield School

Redefield School Hall seen here in 1965.

Redefield Secondary School was built in 1962, occupying a large site along Cuddesdon Way. Its initial in-take was fifty 11 year old pupils and three teachers. David Lewis arrived in May 1963 as headmaster. David Lewis and his long time deputy, Alan Downe, banned corporal punishment and established a detailed pastoral system of discipline that they believed helped save young people from delinquency, and created a caring school atmosphere.

Oxford Schools basketball champions from Redefield School in 1972, completing the season without being beaten. Left to right: Warrell Ramsey, Ian Lewis, Clive Walsh, Paul Parsons, Francis Summersbee, David Jones, Gary Greenaway, Edmund Strzlecki.

1976 left to right back row: Mark Perry, James Perry, Kevin Winter. Sitting: Teresa Lee, Madeleine Dawson, Gillian Lock.

The school grew rapidly, both buildings and numbers of pupils. By September 1967 there were 420 pupils on school roll. The building extensions were not finished and emergency classrooms had to be used. Domestic science lessons were held in the youth club coffee bar - complete with juke box. Other lessons were held in the Community Centre and rooms in Windrush and Evenlode Towers. Classroom population peaked at 845 pupils and 40 teachers, then began to decline.

Redefield hockey girls May 1977 left to right back row: M Dawson, B Moore, S Parker, N Hunt, D Jones, S Howard. Kneeling: A Brandon, S Firkin, J Coffyn, J Paddick, L Harris.

Inside the main hall of Redefield School.

Long distance runner Lynn Harris aged 14 completing the last lap of a 72 hour sponsored marathon at Redefield School in 1978. Classmates and teachers who had run their share of the 3013 lap, 753 mile non-stop marathon were on hand to cheer her home. Twenty pupils and five teachers at the school were involved, to raise £150 for videotapes for the PE department to use for recording sports matches. In 1976, when Mr Neil Angell became head of the PE department, the school staged a 24 hour run. In 1977 it lasted 48 hours, increasing in 1978 to 72 hours.

St John Fisher School

Planting a tree in 1983 in the grounds of St John Fisher School on Sandy Lane West, off the Blackbird Leys fly-over. The school was established to cater for the Catholic children from the estate and nearby areas. Left to right: Mary Finch, Eileen Groom headteacher, Mrs Barresi and baby, Mrs Gaughan, -, -, the Mayoress, -, the Mayor, -, Mr Preston governor, Fr Eddie Butler, Ft Pat Armstong.

Another tree being planted in 1993. Left to right: Darren Gilbey, Kimberley Shafiie-Autery, Louise Dash, -, -Barresi, Michael Tohill.

Shops, Businesses and Public Houses

Balfour Road Shops in August 1960

The first shops, those in Balfour Road, were not built when the first residents moved in. Once the main frame of the building was up, three of the shop keepers set up shop in the garages at the rear - a greengrocers owned for many years by Harry Moakes, a general VG store occupied by the Hills, and a paper shop run by the Thorpe family in the early years. There were no post-office facilities on the estate, the nearest being the Post Office attached to the factory in Hollow Way, Cowley, or the one at Littlemore.

A small general store, with a house attached, was also build on the corner of Sandy Lane and Furlong Close, run for many years by Mr Alf Plaisted, known as 'Big Alf', and then by his daughter. It is now occupied by Mr George Applewhaite.

A mobile shop was set up by Mick Haynes and operated until the late 1970s. This provided essential groceries for the entire estate. It was taken over by Les Allen until 1986, assisted by Christine Gardener. The mobile shop was converted from an old bus and had a metal floor. It was often targetted by youngsters on the estate, and Les solved this problem by befriending the children and giving free easter eggs and small christmas presents to all children under 5. His wife, June Allen, was the longest serving conductress on the Blackbird Leys bus route.

The Blackbird Leys Road parade of shops taken from Windrush Tower. Note the bus stop directly outside the shops. Redefield Library on the grassed corner opposite had still to be built.

Delteys supermarket, at 102/104 Blackbird Leys Road, opened in 1962, owned by Mr L Tidd and his son, Robert, from 1983. Mr Tidd also owned the shop called Roberts in Pegasus Road, now re-opened as Cost Cutters. Mr Durrant was manager of Delteys from 1964 to 1997. The present manager, Paul Whitman, started at the shop in 1971, becoming manager in 1997 and owner in 1998. Johnsons, seen here on the left hand side, was an ironmongers and is now Nash's Bakery. Vidbiz was formerly Motomart, a motor parts shop.

One early shop was Betty's, at 96 Blackbird Leys Road, a popular shop selling wool and haberdashery, as well as children's clothing and underwear. This was owned by Jean West. The shop is now the premises of the Advice Centre.

The Navara Laundrette, also on Blackbird Leys Road, suffered a gas explosion in January 1977, but was quickly back in business.

Staff from Nash's Bakery on Blackbird Leys Road, including manageress, Christine Wood. The staff often dressed up on special occasions including Christmas, Easter and Halloween.

A small garage, a small wooden shack, stood near the bend on Sandy Lane, originally part of the Oxford Greyhound Stadium. This was sold to a Mr Heather some fifteen years ago, and rebuilt in brick. The garage was eventually sold and demolished. The site was redeveloped as a new main entrance for the Stadium.

The Oxford Stadium in Sandy Lane, home to greyhound racing and speedway was originally opened on 31 March 1939, by Lord Denham. The stadium has now been completely rebuilt, but continues to provide local employment.

Public Houses

The Blackbird public house in 1968.

The first public house, aptly named The Blackbird, opened on 13 December 1962, with Ernest and Eileen Hanks as landlords. The original site suggested for a public house had been at the end of Tucker Road, but Peter Malton, the first Priest Missioner, suggested to the Council that it would be better located in the centre of the estate, rather than serve only the patrons of the Stadium. The centre of the estate, around the new public house, was further completed with the laying of turf and the planting of young chestnut trees.

The original Blackbird sign being hoisted up on 11 December 1962. The public house was run by Ind Coope. An off license, facing the main Blackbird Leys Road, operated until renovations were carried out in 1987. Other licensees had included Roger and Margaret Carter from December 1979, taking over from Bill Williams and his wife Doreen who had been there for two years. The licence was transferred to Edward White in 1987.

The Bullnose Morris public house in December 1966.

This was also an Ind Coope Ltd public house. Its name commemorates the 155,000 famous Bullnose Morris motor cars produced at Cowley between 1913 and 1926. The new house was believed to be the only one in the country named after a car. The original plaque, seen here adjacent to the front door, shows the motor car. This plaque has now been removed.

The Bullnose Morris was officially opened in March 1967 by The Lord Mayor of Oxford, Councillor Air Vice-Marshall W F MacNeece Foster. Ken Revis, president of the Bullnose Morris Club, formally declared the pub open and draw the first pint, which was presented to the Lord Mayor. Licensees in 1984 were David and Penny Vaughan.

Sports, Activities and Events

Blackbird Gymnasts

Mr Robin Cox joined the staff of Blackbird Leys County Primary School in 1962. He started a school gymn club just after Christmas 1963. Original members included Beverley Chandler and Noreen Collins. The Blackbird Gymnasts, as they became known, were very successful, appearing on children's television, The Blue Peter Programme, several times, the first time on 20 December 1965, shown above: left to right back row David Harwood aged 11, Jenny Weaving 10, Gaynor Coolman 11, Calvin Goodgame 11. Front row: Marlene Williams 9, Gloria Constant 9, Debra Clark 10, Lorraine Harwood 10, Catherine Evans 10. Lorraine Harwood, Gloria Constant and Paula Stone had finished 5th 6th and 7th in the girls' individual competition for the South of England Tumbling championships in 1962. Eleven year old Calvin Goodgame was 7th in the boys competition.

David Williams, aged 10, was a talented gymnast. Only a few boys joined the gymnast club, but David, known as Widge, maintained his interest for many years. He was a Southern Area Champion by the age of 11 and made regular appearances on the *Blue Peter* television programme. David continued to compete until the age of 20, at which time he trained at Radley College.

1970s photos of the Blackbird Gymnasts, displaying medals won at the Champions of Great Britain contest at Darlington. Left to right back row: Coaches Robin Cox, John Honey, Bill Harwood, Ron Hookham, Dave Lock. Middle row: Catherine Evans, Susan French, Lorraine Harwood, Carol Taylor. Front row: Debbie Clark, Petrina Hookham. Mr Bill Harwood succeeded Robin Cox as club manager, and ran the club, with help from Mr McDonald, for many years.

The Blackbird Leys Boys Football Team was first formed in 1961. This first team comprised, left to right back row: Tony Tompkins, Alan Norwood, Tony Wheeler, David Cook, Norman Evans, -. Front row: Mick Mazurek, Roger Deacon, Brian Cook, Robert Dean, Terry Waite. The manager at this time was Arthur Cook.

In Arthur Cook's garden in Sawpit Road, c1962. Left to right back row: Arthur Cook manager, John-, Norman Evans, David Beament, Tony Wheeler, Alan Norwood, Tony Tompkins, -. Kenny Souch(?) at back. Front row: Mick Mazurek, Roger Deacon, Brian Cook, Robert Dean, Terry Waite.

The boys team in 1966/67. Left to right back row: Mr G Walker, Rober White, Henry O'Connor, Chris Amor, David Blackmore, Paul Godrey, David Parrot, Mr Joe Mazurek manager. Front row: Alan Richards, J Perella, J Parry, A Walker, Clive Brammell, Neil Hartigan, Clive Young.

One young player, Roger White, emigrated to Australia c1966 and a special presentation was made to him by the rest of the team. Roger White in middle being presented by Johnny Creighton of Oxford United, with manager, Joe Mazurek, on the right, Joe Mazurek was manager of the team for many years. He was a Polish immigrant who had originally travelled to Cowley to find work in the Pressed Steel factory. Many men of Polish extraction were based at Checkenden, a de-mob camp for the Polish army, and many of these people, with their families, were rehoused on the new Blackbird Leys estate.

The Blackbird Leys Boys teams grew in strength and eventually catered for many age groups. The above photograph is of the 13, 14 and 15 year old teams in c1967. Left to right back row: Bob Perry, David Cook, Tony Tomkins, Melvin Moss, John Saxton, Steve Slatter, Paul Giles, Mick Mazurek, Andy Jackson, John Bingham, Shaun Mulvanney. Next row: ~, ~, Ian Buckett, ~, Tony Perrella, ~, John Beale, ~, ~, Robert Finch, Billy Beeches, Greg Renshaw, ~, Robert Dean, ~, Clive Brandrom. Next row: Henry O'Connor, David Blackmore, Clive Young, Nickie Burden, Roger White, Steve Gossen, ~Hall, ~, ~, Chris Drewett, ~, ~, Paul Godfrey, Simon Massey, Nigel Smith, Steve Kenny. Front row: ~, John Parry, John Perrella, Andy Walker, David Parrot, Brendon O'Connor, Andy Richards. Left group: ~, Joe Mazurek, George Gatt, ~, in front unknown representative from Heinz who presented the trophies. Right hand side group: Gordon Walker, Arthur Cook, Johnny Creighton, 'Flash' the trainer. Cyril Beavan of Oxford United seated in front.

Blackbird Leys school football team in 1967, after winning their first trophy. Having lost in three finals in 1966, the team finally 'made it' when they defeated St Nicholas, Old Marston 1-0, scored by centre forward Steve Godfrey, to win the Oxford Schools' Juniior League Shield. Left to right back row: Richard Forrest, Graeme Young, Dsau Slezec, Gordon Peel, -Mitchell?, Mark Ludbrooke, Mathew Smith. Front row: Martin Turley, Gary Rodregez, Chris Anderson, Pete Mitchell, Simon Mayell, Steve Godfrey, Paul Saxton.

The Under 16/17s and Under 18s, in dark shirts, from the Youth Club c1967, left to right back row: George Buckett, manager under 16/17, Paul Giles, Les Buckett, Terry Waite, Roger Deacon, Dave Buck, Brian Cook, Steve Slatter, Dave Mitchell, manager Joe Williamson. Middle row: Alastair Black, John Brown, John Mastroddi, Norman Evans, Jimmy Kearey, Andy Glass, John Saxton. Front row: Dave Quinn, Ian Buckett, -, Robin Godfrey.

The youth club Under 19s in the early 1960s. Joe Williamson on the left was manager for many years.

Social Club 1972 outing to Holland. Left to right back row: John Spain, Herbie Payne, Peter Courtnage, George Carnegie. Back: -, Terry Waite, Eddie Courtnage, John Weaver, Mick Chapman. Front: Bob Drewitt, Ricky Mansell, Les Buckett.

Pool team from The Blackbird in 1977, at the Southern Final Elimination in London. Back row left to right: Ted Carton captain, Tony Webb landlord, Duncan Naish, Billy Beeches, Gordon Collier, Geoff Tombs, Les Gaul, Anton Bazylkiewicz.

Hillend campers in 1961, outside 'The Blue Dragon'.

Many activities took place during those early years at Blackbird Leys School, but particularly memorable are the annual camps at Hillend at Wytham (40 children in 1960 - 120 in 1964)'Peel. Staff from Blackbird Leys County Primary School involved in school camps in the 1960s and early 1970s included: Cecil Jacobs, David Munday, Robin Cox, Gordon Peel, Roy Money, Ray Wyman, Tony Davies, Nigel Simpson, Robin Winstone, Margaret Peel (nee Macdiarmiad), Eunice Rummings, Lucy Cox, Hilary Catchpole, Hilary Wright, Joyce Hamill, Barbara Wharton, Margaret Tatton, Rosemary Marshall.

Winners of Hillend Scavenger Hunt, 1961. Left to right back row: -, Charles Unwin, -. Front row: Carole Young, Sandra Jordan, Angela Cooke, -.

Hillend Campers c1962, back row left to right: Linda Minchin, -, -, Robert Dean, Lorraine Kinch, -, Marion Bromley, -, Lesley Godfrey?, -, -. Middle row: Stephen Gossen, -, -, -. In front: -, -, -.

Hillend camp in 1966 includes: left to right back row: Eva Fleet, -, -, -. Next row: -, -, June Bowen, -, Marina Barrett. Girls sitting: -Cherry, -, -, -, Sharon Bennett, Valerie Porter, Maureen Jacobs, Pamela Berry, Betty Roberts, Jane Hodnett, Susan John. Front row: -Brandish, -, -, -, -, Gary Sawyer, -, -, -.

Retirement of Gordon and Margaret Peel in 1990.

Margaret and Gordon Peel, between them, worked at Wesley Green Middle School for fifty five years. They met in 1960 and were married three years later. Gordon was responsible for setting up and running the schools computer network, and was always active in school sports. Margaret helped set up the first after-school club in 1960, and took a major role in the school's drama productions. Left to right back row: Marg Jerrett, Ann Cardwell, Rachel Kenyon, Louise Wilson, Jean-, Ruth Minott, -. Next row: Mrs Parish, Evelyn Floyd, Shirley Bowler, -. Next row: Nicky Stokes, Joyce Hamell, Dee St Claire, Shirley Mackenzie, Margaret Ward, Keith Talent, Audrey Clarke, Carol Pether. Front row: Heather Wilson, Mr Wyman, Teresa Oak, Gordon Peel, Margaret Peel, Peter Roper, Ann Brewer, Ann Callahan.

In 1991 Mavis Harris retired after 25 years as 'lolly-pop lady' for Wesley Green school, seen here with a group of children on Balfour Road at the junction with Sawpit Road. Longlands Old People's Home is in the middle of the photograph.

On 3 August 1976 there was a disastrous fire at, what was now, Shepherds' Hill School, which destroyed four classrooms. This incident was remembered by Mrs Joyce Hamill who worked at the school as a teacher for 22 years, from 1967 when it was Blackbird Leys Junior School, until her official retirement as Leader of Year 6 in 1989. She immediately returned as a voluntary support teacher.

11 July 1980 saw the retirement of three head teachers. Cecil Jacobs, on the left, had been head of Blackbird Leys School, later named Shepherds' Hill, since it opened in 1959. Miss Pam Drury, centre, was head of Orchard Meadow First School since it opened as an infants school in 1961, and Mr Jimmy James head of Overmede First School since it opened in 1965.

The inscription on the church font was arranged by Cecil Jacobs and officially presented in June 1981 in commemoration of his 21 years as headmaster of Blackbird Leys School. The inscription was a palindrome in Greek which, when read either way, says the same thing - 'NIYONANOMHMATAMHMONANOYIN' - meaning *wash my transgressions, not only my face.*

Retirement of five teachers from Redefield at the time of closure in 1982. Left to right: David Lewis, Eileen Gould, Bert Newman, Pat Chantry and Roy Keen.

In 1982 it was announced that Redefield School was to close on 16 July. By 24 June 1982 only a handful of pupils were left, to finish O level courses. Redefield was the first comprehensive school to close in Oxford. David Lewis, the headteacher, had been in charge for all but two terms.

The Redefield Sports Hall, on Pegasus Road, was built in the late 1960s, primarily for school use, but with public facilities for indoor football, basket ball and squash. After the closure of Redefield School the facilities remained for the community. The building was upgraded in 1989 to provide more space for sports, together with changing rooms, a conference room, a small hall and separate meeting rooms. A plaque to commemorate the extension work was unveiled by Mrs Barbara Gatehouse, chairman of Oxford City Council Recreation and Amenities Committee.

The school buildings were taken over by the College of Further Education on 23 July 1982. The College used some old classrooms for gas fitting, motor vehicle maintenance and electrical installation courses. Northfield Special School, at the end of Knights Road, temporarily took over a teaching block and Wesley Green Middle School used the gym and home economics room.

The original police houses on the corner of Cuddesdon Way and Sawpit Road seen here in 1991. Empty for many years these have now been converted into the very successful Cuddesdon Corner Family Centre.

The beginnings of the Adventure Playground on Cuddesdon Way.

The Adventure Playground was officially opened in 1991, with the Wesley Green school steele band seen here.

Spindleberry Park
The reservoir within Spindleberry Park. The park, between Pegasus Road and Northfield Brook, was developed as a nature park, incorporating the original reservoir that can be seen on the map of 1899, pages 6 and 7. Years ago the reservoir was home to masses of rud fish and is still a popular place for local children.

Children fishing at 'the reservoir'.

The BMX track within Spindleberry Park was started in March 1983 and attracted many members. A formal club, called The Hotshots, with membership fees and strict rules, was formed by local residents and run by Eileen Clements for many years.

Floods

The Cook family at 32 Blackbird Leys Road, where more than seventy homes were flooded with water four feet deep.

On 14 July 1967 there was a very violent thunderstorm, starting about ten at night. Rain was torrential and the earth, baked hard from a hot summer, did not immediately drain away. Drains could not cope with the volume of water and the 'dip' at the bottom of Blackbird Leys Road, on the corner of Balfour Road, was totally flooded. Manhole covers were forced up and water was fouled with untreated sewage. The torrential rain was compounded by a burst water main in Furlong Close. The Community Centre was opened by Rev Mervyn Puleston and Warden Frith, and emergency camp beds were set up. Following the flood, Councillor Maureen Coombes, of 60 Kestrel Crescent, launched a flood fund. Fifty homes had been severely damaged, numbers 9 to 31 Blackbird Leys Road being the hardest hit.

During the following week pupils at Redefield School helped local pensioners to retrieve furniture and attempted to dry carpets.

During May 1968 a local 16 year girl, Glenis Parrott of Sandy Lane, won the Miss Greyhound Racing Competition, a prestigious national event. Glenis was a dog parader for many years, also working at the local training kennels, which used to be situated behind the garage.

Pegasus Court, at the corner of Cuddesdon Way and Pegasus Road, was built in 1973 by North Cheshire Housing Association. The flats experienced problems with ventalation, condensation and damp and were finally demolished in the summer of 1998.

A new development of 69 houses and flats was built on the site by Ealing Family Housing Association. The block - Olive Whister Court - was named after a popular and active resident, and was officially opened by Val Smith.

During the early 1990s Blackbird Leys suffered a great deal from joy-riders, exacerbated by crowds of onlookers, many of whom were not from the estate. This, together with the surrounding publicity and almost nightly police presence, gave the estate a very bad reputation. The church wished to reinforce the positive aspects of the estate and the residents, and Rev. James Ramsay organised a community service of reconciliation, which was preceded by the release of a huge number of balloons with messages from the children in support of 'their' estate. This was held on the grass opposite the Blackbird Leys shops.

Prince Charles paid a visit to the estate during 1994 and this greatly helped to remove the stigma suffered by the estate for several years. Left to right: Jean Peach, Audrey John (back of head), Phyllis Arnold, -, -.

A resident who has lived in Moorbank since 1960 recalls the day of the visit: '*a lady walked by, in a hurry to see Prince Charles who was outside the church. I offered her a rose from my front garden and was amazed to see later, on TV, that same lady give the rose the Charles. He wore it for the rest of his visit.*'

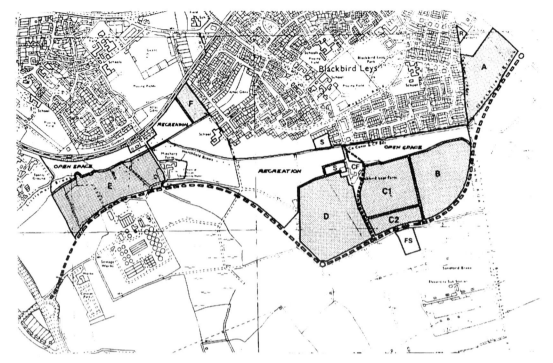

The first development on remaining farmland to the east of Blackbird Leys began in 1985. However, the development had to be severely reduced in size because of government cuts and spending control, allowing only site 'A' to be completed along Grenoble Road, a new perimeter road off the Watlington Road. This development remained in isolation for many years, with no local shops or public transport. Pedestrian walkways connected the 'old' estate with this new part. A minibus service operated a half-hourly service between Monday and Saturday 8a.m. to 6p.m.

Skylark Close, originally known as Kestrel Close and later Kestrel Place, off Kestrel Crescent, before the development of Area F, and what became the Falcon Close area.

The development of Grenoble Road, to accommodate the new part of the estate, which became known as Greater Leys. Tony Williamson, chairman of Blackbird Leys Development Committee, and Mr Herbie Payne, resident representative, turned the first sod on 2 May 1987.

Windale School, a new First School, was built at the bottom of Windale Avenue to accommodate children moving into the new development. The school was opened by Jeremy Irons on Friday 8 March 1996, seen here with headteacher, Christine Lewin and Tony Williamson.

By 1990 Oxford's housing needs had become so acute that the city council realised the only solution was to develop the green field land on the outskirts of the city - a development that became known in the media as Greater Leys. The chosen site was part of the former Blackbird Leys Farm, which the council owned, and the entire site was to provide 1700 new homes. The first 400 of these, being within Phase 1, were built in the early 1990s.

Blackbird Leys School photograph 1965 (inside back cover)

Left to right back row: 8 girls unknown, Carolyn Taylor, -, -Howard, Peter Lennon, -, -, Edward Parker, Graeme Young, 6 girls unknown, Ann Kenny, James Felix, -, -, -, -, Peter Hopkins, -, Nancy Taylor.

Jimmy Hillis, Paul Saxton, -, Wayne Franklin, Susan French, -, -, Stephen Penny, 6 girls unknown, Robert Waller, 3 girls unknown, Sharon Whiteman, -, 4 boys unknown, Stephen Godfrey, 2 girls unknown, Simon Mayall, Christopher Dandridge, -, 3 boys unknown, Gary Maybee, Ronald Barber, Peter Rowland, Richard Day, -, -, Stephen Bucket, Julian Bazylkiewicz, 4 girls unknown, Karen West, -, Karen Webb, Maureen Collington, Myra Howley, -, Jane Greenaway, Audrey Deans, 4 girls unknown, -, Gregory Fleet, Ronald-, Paul Bellinger, Melania Slezak, Pam Williams, -, David Elsmore, Stuart McCartney.

-Chandler, 12 boys unknown, David Booth, Cherell Bradbury, 4 girls unknown, Carol-, 5 girls unknown, -Aston, 2 girls unknown, 2 boys unknown, Francis King, 2 boys unknown, Charlie Perry, -, -, Helen-, Stephen Kenny, -, Deborah Thompson, Roy Stephens, Michael Keene, -, Edward Cothier, -, Stephen Spiers, Mark Merry, Michael Collington, Angela Davis, Angela Tompkins, -, Alan Thompson, Christopher Sawyer, Susan Smith, 2 girls unknown, Joan Brackett, Martin Harris, -, Mark Risbrooke, -, -, David Belcher, Judith O'Loughlin, Ann-, Lorina Taylor.

2 boys unknown, Gloria Constance, Mark Ludbrook, Steve Mason, -, Raymond Edge, Paul Robson, Dsau Sledjak, -, Neale Spencer, 2 boys unknown, John McIntyre, David Norwood, -, Gary McCrowan, -, Lewis Boroky, Debra Copeland, Christine Brooks, 2 girls unknown, Gail Mason, Beverley Garfitt, 2 girls unknown, -Cothier, -, -Steele, 2 girls unknown, -, Paul Hurrell, John Chandler, Ian Lawson, Miriam Herman, -, David Wheeler, Eileen Hubbie, -, -Hill, David Woodley, Clive Harding, Edmund Coles, Claire Halewood, Adrian Summersbee, Carol Matthews, Dorothy Edwards, Linda Smith, -Brain, Paul Irons, -Toombes, June Murphy, Catherine Evans, Phillip-, Stephen Mott, -, Carol Walton, Deborah Johnson, Stephen Organ, -Chandler, Graham Johnson, Rita Benfield, Susan Wilkins.

2 boys unknown, -, Susan Haynes, John Cadd, Brian Kemp, Jeremy Barber, Julie Bowen, Trevor Martin, 2 girls unknown, Malcolm Heath, -, Alan Stole, Suzanne Williams, -, -, Janice Phipps, Matthew Smith, -, Sandra Wyatt, -, -, -Greenaway, -, Geoff Wyman, -, John Haines, Steven Fowler, Mark Wyatt, -, Pat Wyatt, -, June Haines, Susan Hodnett, 5 girls unknown, Susan Harris, Virginia-, -, Karen Green, -Bednarz?, 4 girls unknown, -, Stephen Morris, 2 girls unknown, -, Julia Cook, Amanda Clark, Lorraine Harwood, Stephen Barrett, Valerie Moorcroft, -Harwood, Gordon Holloway, Susan McAvoy.

Peter Blake, John Solomon, Cheryl Evans, Glen-, Barbara Clibbon, Steven Grubey, Cynthia Welch, Lester Bradbury, Brian Tobin, Richard Hastie, -, Elaine Dean, -, Nigel Clark, Freddie Bentley, Shelagh Murphy, Phillip-, -, -, Janet Fernhill, Virginia Jerrett, Christine Lacey, Paul Hackle, Ermine Lewis, Jennifer Beaumont, Teresa Mazurek,

Geoff Buckett, Martin Robson, Ken Howard, David-, Sally Willett, Danuta Bednarz, -, Steve Green, -, Stuart Partlett, David Warne, Ann Fitzpatrick, David-, Jackie White, John Godwin, Barbara Waller, Michael-, Glynnis Johns, Christopher Matthews, William Cothier, Julie-, Martin Long, Susan Smith, Barry Williams, Dorothy Martin, Paul Bowerman, Susan Tyrrell, Monnie Perry, -, Linda Higgs, Yvonne Reeve, Kevin Portsmouth, Elaine Arnold, Ray Ward.

-, Debra Phipps, Eddie Greenaway, 2 girls unknown, Pauline-, 2 boys unknown, -, Kevin Jones, David Horwood, Clive Young, Stephen Greenaway, -, Desde Holland. Teachers: Robin Cox, Avril Banton, David Munday, -, Mrs Nicholls, -, Elaine Brown, 3 unknown, Valerie Lucas, Cecil Jacobs head master, Rosemary Marshall, 2 unknown, Roy Money, Miss Barrier, Nigel Simpson, Sue Dykes, Gordon Peel (end of teachers row). Elaine Turton, -, Neil Taylor, Jane-, -, Pauline Kynnersley, Amanda Steele, David Orman, Paul Day, -, Warwick Clifton, John Cooper, Selina Aston, -, Eddie Beeches, Deborah Harris, James Weir?

Gary Thomas, 2 girls unknown, Maureen Jacobs, Jane Godfrey, Sandra Pritchard, 4 girls unknown, -, Kim Holmes, Adrian Spiers, -Brain, Mick Hall, 3 boys unknown, Brian King, -, Arlene Harris, Jane Hinton, Marie Barrett, -, Gary Watts, Caroline Reeves, Valerie Porter, 2 girls unknown, Judith Boyce, Pamela Berry, -, Jane Hodnett, Beverley Montague, -, Adrian Rook, -, -, Julie Clifton, Jennifer Swanton, Patsie Trubey, Jane Gardner, -, Pat Martin, Barry Godfrey, -, Vanessa Clinton, 2 girls unknown, Jane-, Elaine-, Yvetta Cimmernanis, Christopher Eeley, 2 girls unknown, -, -, Andrew 'Jammie' Robinson, 2 boys unknown, Carl Buckingham, Marie Batts, -, Shaun Jones, Karen Gomm, Mickie Taylor, -, Arthur Cooke.

Jennifer Adams, Gary Thomas, Pete Barrett, Martin Smith, Kevin Peeper, -, Rodwell Solomon, Paul Brough, -, Gloria Perks, Nadine Hill, Karen Rand, Colin Dawson, Colin Yeoman, Susan Brooks, Kim Johnson, -, Stephen Chamberlain, -, Sheila Morris, Stephen Whipp, Christine Laney, Pat Dash, Simon Cotterill, Helen Moor, Shirley Beeches, Lois King, Carol Montague, Stephen Bennett, -, Martin Penny, -, Jane Johnson, -, 2 boys unknown, -, 2 boys unknown, -, Michael Smith, Carol Felix, -, Brenda Cherry, -, Deborah Cothier, -, -Murphy, Alwyn Jones, -, Paul Harris, -Stephens, -, -, 2 girls unknown, 2 boys unknown, Anthony Tompkins, Gary Tolley, Lorraine Pritchard.

Linda Benfield, Sharon Barrett, Alan Cox, Colin Smith, -, Michael Chapman, Denise Hurrell, -, Michael Herbert, Stuart Neilson, Lindsey Neilson, June Bowen, Trevor Rodregez, Carol Boucher, Jennifer Turford, Marilyn Hilsdon, Linda Walton, Georgie Hicks, Linda Brown, Ian Dawson, Betty Roberts, -, Tony Herman, Ian Hill, Vivienne Brooks, -, John Herman, -, Carl Rackley, John Ewers, Sharon Mason, -, Caroline Stevens, Sue Cooke, Mark Thompson, -, -, Nicholas Matthews, John Reid, Alan Bennett, -, Melvin Johnson, Caroline Reeves, -, Debrah Sawyer, Terry Winstone, Bobby Maybee, Christine Norriss, Julia Kimber, Christine-, Teresa Green, Lorraine Coplin, Phillip Horwood, Marie Thompson, Francine King, Peter Brackett.